BOSTON COMMON PRESS
Brookline, Massachusetts

2000

Other titles in the *Cook's Illustrated*
How to Cook Series

HOW TO COOK CHICKEN BREASTS

An illustrated step-by-step guide to
foolproof grilled, broiled, roasted,
sautéed, baked, and stir-fried
chicken breasts and cutlets.

THE COOK'S ILLUSTRATED LIBRARY

Illustrations by John Burgoyne

Boston Common Press
17 Station Street
Brookline, Massachusetts 02445

ISBN 0-936184-47-7
Library of Congress Cataloging-in-Publication Data
The Editors of *Cook's Illustrated*
How to cook chicken breasts: An illustrated step-by-step guide to foolproof grilled, broiled, roasted, sautéed, baked, and stir-fried chicken breasts and cutlets./The Editors of *Cook's Illustrated*
1st ed.

Includes 44 recipes and 15 illustrations
ISBN 0-936184-47-7 (hardback): $14.95
I. Cooking. I. Title
2000

Manufactured in the United States of America

Distributed by Boston Common Press, 17 Station Street, Brookline, MA 02445.

Cover and text design: Amy Klee
Recipe development: Elizabeth Germain
Series editor: Jack Bishop

CONTENTS

introduction

I T's NO SECRET THAT MOST AMERICANS PREFER white meat to dark meat chicken. Meat from the breast is lean and tender and can be delicious, but because white meat contains very little fat, it can be tricky to cook. The recipes in this book are designed to keep moisture in while cooking delicate breasts.

For instance, most everyone has had grilled bone-in breasts that were charred on the exterior and bloody near the bone. After extensive testing, we found that bone-in breasts are best seared over a hot fire, then moved to a cool part of the grill to cook through.

Broiling is a great alternative to grilling, especially in the winter months. But too often the kitchen fills with smoke before broiled breasts are cooked through to the bone. We found that the secret to perfectly broiled breasts is keeping the chicken far from the heating element (about 13 inches is just right) until nearly done, then moving the pan up closer to the broiler to brown the skin. In addition, our test cooks found that slashing the skin before broiling is key to supercrisp skin.

Sautéed cutlets can be delicious if done right. But too often they emerge from the pan tough and poorly browned. Our testing revealed that an extremely hot skillet, the right fat (in this case, vegetable oil), and proper timing are essential when sautéing cutlets.

In addition to proper cooking methods, we found that brining—soaking chicken breasts in a saltwater solution— helps to retain moisture in this delicate meat. (For more information on the science of brining, see page 10.) This extra step does add some time to recipes, but the results make brining well worth the wait.

How to Cook Chicken Breasts is the 25th book in the How to Cook series published by *Cook's Illustrated,* a bimonthly publication on American home cooking. Turn to the beginning of the book for a complete list of the titles in the series. To order other books, call us at (800) 611-0759 or visit us online at www.cooksillustrated.com. For a free trial copy of *Cook's,* call (800) 526-8442.

Christopher P. Kimball
Publisher and Editor
Cook's Illustrated

chapter one

≋

CHICKEN BASICS

THIS CHAPTER COVERS A NUMBERS OF BASIC issues concerning the purchase and preparation of chicken, including the differences between cutlets and breasts, the purpose of brining, and the importance of proper, safe handling.

BREASTS OR CUTLETS?

If you like white meat, you have two basic choices: breasts with the bone in and skin on, or cutlets, breasts from which the bones and skin have been removed. If you buy breasts, you can purchase them whole or split. The former is the entire breast taken from a single chicken. Split

8

breasts are basically whole breasts that have been halved along the breastbone.

Cutlets are split breasts that are taken off the bone and skinned. Most cutlets contain the main portion of the breast plus a long, skinny piece of meat that runs along the side of the bird. This flap of meat, which is attached to the underside of the cutlet, is called the tenderloin. If you see packages of cutlets marked "thinly sliced" or "trimmed," the tenderloins may have been removed. Except in the case of grilling, when the added thickness of the tenderloin slows down the cooking process too much, we prefer to buy regular cutlets, with the tenderloins still attached. These cutlets are thicker, so it's easier to retain their juices during cooking.

When purchasing a package of breasts, you will find a wide variation in size. In shopping to develop the recipes for this book, we found bone-in split breasts that weighed from 7 to 14 ounces. If you try to roast or grill small and large breasts at the same time, you will need to make some adjustments in the cooking time, removing smaller pieces from the heat first. We find it easier to buy breasts that are all the same size, preferably 10 to 12 ounces.

Cutlets can range in size from 4 to 10 ounces. Again, you will make your work much easier if you try to buy medium-sized cutlets, each weighing about 6 ounces. Excess fat should be removed, as should the tough, white tendon that runs through the tenderloin (see figures 1 and 2 on pages 12 and 13 for details).

THE PURPOSE OF BRINING

Because breasts and cutlets are so lean, we find that they can often dry out. This can be especially problematic when cooking cutlets by dry heat methods such as grilling, broiling, or roasting. (Cutlets cooked in plenty of fat or liquid are less likely to dry out.) In these cases, we like to brine chicken breasts and cutlets.

We find that soaking chicken parts in a saltwater solution before cooking keeps the meat juicier. Brining also gives delicate (and sometimes mushy) chicken a meatier, firmer consistency and seasons the meat right to the center of the cut.

How does brining work? Brining actually promotes a change in the structure of the proteins that make up a muscle. The salt causes protein strands to unwind, in a process called *denaturing*, just as they do when exposed to heat, acid, or alcohol. When protein strands unwind, they get tangled in one another and trap water in the matrix that forms. Salt is commonly used to give processed meats a better texture. For example, hot dogs made without salt would be limp.

Brining time is varied depending on the size of the chicken parts. For instance, we found that bone-in, skin-on breasts should be brined for 1½ hours but that boneless, skinless cutlets become nicely plumped and seasoned after just 45 minutes.

We often add sugar to the brine. The sugar does not affect the texture of the meat, but it does add flavor. For instance, we find that brining chicken breasts in a sugar-salt solution enhances the caramelization (or browning) that occurs when the parts are grilled, thereby also enhancing flavor. Because brined chicken browns more quickly than nonbrined chicken, it is important to watch it carefully as it cooks.

Note that we have listed kosher or regular table salt in recipes that call for brining. Because of the difference in the size of the crystals, cup for cup, table salt is about twice as strong as kosher salt.

SAFE HANDLING

Given the prevalence of bacteria in the poultry supply in this country, it's probably best to assume that the chicken you buy is contaminated. That means you need to follow some simple rules to minimize the danger to you and your family.

Keep chicken refrigerated until just before cooking. Bacteria thrive at temperatures between 40 and 140 degrees. This means leftovers should also be promptly refrigerated.

When handling poultry, make sure to wash hands, knives, cutting boards, and counters (or anything else that has come into contact with the raw chicken, its juices, or your hands) with hot, soapy water. Be especially careful not to let the chicken, its juices, or your hands touch foods (like salad ingredients) that will be eaten raw.

Finally, cook chicken breasts and cutlets to an internal temperature of 160 degrees to ensure that any bacteria have been killed. Use an instant-read thermometer to gauge when chicken is done. Note that cooking white meat chicken to temperatures much above 160 degrees will cause juices to be lost and will result in drier, less appealing meat.

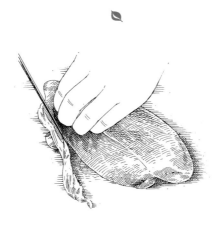

Figure 1.
Lay each cutlet tenderloin-side down and smooth the top with your fingers. Any fat will slide to the periphery, where it can be trimmed with a knife.

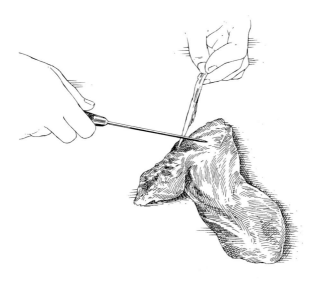

Figure 2.
To remove the tough, white tendon, turn the cutlet tenderloin-
side up and peel back the thick half of the tenderloin so it lies top
down on the work surface. Use the point of a paring knife
to cut around the top of the tendon to expose it, then
scrape the tendon free with the knife.

chapter two

GRILLED BREASTS & CUTLETS

B ONE-IN, SKIN-ON BREASTS AND BONELESS, skinless cutlets can both be grilled, but each requires its own methods for flavoring and cooking.

GRILLED BREASTS

Grilled chicken breasts should have richly caramelized, golden brown (not burnt) skin and moist, juicy meat. With very little fat, breasts have a tendency to dry out. The fact that many bone-in breasts can be more than an inch thick doesn't help. The skin can char and the exterior layers of meat can dry out by the time the meat near the bone is cooked through.

14

We divided our tests on grilled chicken breasts into three sets. The first involved partial cooking off the grill; the second involved particular ways of moving the chicken around on the grill surface, as well as use of the grill cover for part of the cooking time; and the third involved various ways of treating the chicken before cooking it, both to add flavor and to improve texture.

We had thought that some of the methods of partially cooking the chicken off the grill would work pretty well, but we were wrong. Poaching the chicken before grilling resulted in dry chicken with a cottony texture. Microwaving prior to grilling was even worse: The chicken ended up not only dry but rubbery, and the skin failed to crisp despite its postmicrowave time on the grill.

Our next approach was to sear the breasts on the grill first, then finish the cooking off the grill. Using the microwave to finish cooking after a five-minute sear on the grill wasn't bad, and it is acceptable for those times when you're in a hurry to get food on the table. Unlike the chicken that was microwaved before being grilled, these pieces had crispy skin, and the meat was evenly cooked throughout. But the meat was also slightly less juicy than that cooked entirely on the grill.

Our final attempt at combined cooking methods came even closer to the goal. Again we seared the breasts on the grill but this time finished cooking them in a 350-degree oven. The meat was evenly cooked and remained juicy, with none of the toughness experienced with other combined cooking methods; the skin, which had crisped up nicely during its time on the grill, remained quite crisp after its sojourn in the oven.

The differences between this method and our final favorite were differences of degree. The meat was just slightly less tender, the skin a bit less crispy. More important, this oven method used two different appliances and required you to do part of the cooking outside on the grill and the rest in the kitchen. Not only was this needlessly cumbersome, it was also less fun, given that part of the appeal of grilling is standing around the fire while sipping your favorite beverage and passing the time of day as you cook. So we consigned this method to the reject pile along with the other, less successful combination cooking techniques.

We next moved on to test methods that involved cooking on the grill alone. Each involved some variation on a two-level fire, that is, a fire in which one area of the grill is hotter than the other. The idea in every case was to get the sear from the hotter fire and cook the chicken evenly all the way through over the cooler part of the grill.

The first of these methods seemed particularly contrary, but a friend had insisted that it worked, so we gave it a test run. In this method, the chicken was cooked on a low fire first, then finished up on a hot fire. Like microwaving, however, this backward approach resulted in dry meat—a lame result for a method that saved no time or energy.

Next we tried the method that intuitively seemed most likely to succeed: searing the chicken breasts over the coals and then moving them to a cool part of the grill to finish cooking. The breasts refused to cook through to the bone in less than half an hour. By this time the skin was burning and the outer layers of meat were dry. We tried using the grill cover but detected some off flavors from the burned-on ashes that had built up on the inside of the cover. (This ash buildup is a common problem with charcoal grilling but not gas grilling, in which the fire burns much more cleanly.)

We did notice, however, that cooking with the cover cut the grilling time back to 20 minutes. Less time over the flames meant the skin was not black and the meat was still juicy. We decided to improvise a cover by using a disposable aluminum roasting pan (an old restaurant trick) to build up heat around the breasts and help speed along the cooking. After searing for five minutes, we moved the breasts to a cooler part of the fire, covered them with a disposable pan, and continued grilling for another 15 minutes or so. This allowed the breasts to cook through without burning.

It was now time to consider ways of adding flavor to the

chicken. Options included marinades, spice rubs and pastes, barbecue sauces, salsas, and brining.

Marinating the chicken was disappointing. Even several hours in a classic oil-and-acid marinade added only a small amount of flavor to the finished chicken, and oil dripping off the marinated chicken caused constant flare-ups during the initial searing period.

Rubbing the chicken with a spice rub prior to grilling proved far more satisfactory. Because rubs and pastes are composed almost entirely of spices, they have enough flavor intensity to stand up to the smoky grilled flavor of the meat. Barbecue sauces often contain some sweetener and can burn if brushed on the chicken before cooking. We found it best to brush them on when cooking was almost done, serving extra sauce at the table, if desired. You can also skip flavoring the chicken with a rub or sauce and instead serve it with a salsa or chutney.

As a final test, we tried brining the chicken before grilling it. We tried brining for various amounts of time and found that by using a brine with a high concentration of salt and sugar, we could achieve the result we wanted in only 1½ hours. The brine penetrated the chicken to the bone, seasoning it and helping to firm up its texture before grilling.

♛

Master Recipe

Charcoal-Grilled Bone-In Chicken Breasts

serves four

➤ **NOTE**: *If the fire flares because of dripping fat or a gust of wind, move the chicken to the area of the grill without coals until the flames die down. Brining improves the chicken's flavor, but if you're short on time, skip step 1 and season the chicken generously with salt as well as pepper before cooking. Add flavorings before or during cooking: Rub the chicken parts with a spice rub or paste (pages 23–24) before they go on the grill, or brush them with barbecue sauce during the final 2 minutes of cooking (see page 21).*

¾ **cup kosher salt or 6 tablespoons table salt**

¾ **cup sugar**

4 **split chicken breasts (bone in, skin on), 10 to 12 ounces each, excess fat and skin trimmed (see figure 3, page 22)**

Ground black pepper

Disposable aluminum roasting pan

⁂ INSTRUCTIONS:

1. Dissolve salt and sugar in 1 quart cold water in gallon-sized, zipper-lock plastic bag. Add chicken; press out as much air as possible from bag and seal; refrigerate until fully seasoned, about 1½ hours.

2. Light large chimney starter filled with charcoal and allow to burn until charcoal is covered with layer of fine gray ash. Build a two-level fire by stacking all coals on one side of grill (see figure 4, page 22). Set cooking rack in place, cover grill with lid, and let rack heat up, about 5 minutes. Use wire brush to scrape clean cooking rack.

3. Meanwhile, remove chicken from brine, rinse well, dry thoroughly with paper towels, and season with pepper to taste or with one of the spice rubs or pastes on pages 23 and 24.

4. Cook chicken, uncovered, over hotter part of grill until well browned, 2 to 3 minutes per side. Move chicken to cooler part of grill and cover with disposable aluminum roasting pan; continue to cook, skin-side up, for 10 minutes. Turn and cook for 5 minutes more or until done. To test for doneness, either peek into thickest part of chicken with tip of small knife (you should see no redness near the bone) or check internal temperature at thickest part with instant-read thermometer, which should register 160 degrees. Transfer to serving platter. Serve hot or at room temperature.

:: VARIATIONS:

Gas-Grilled Bone-In Chicken Breasts

With the lid down on a gas grill, there's no need to cook the chicken under a disposable roasting pan.

Follow master recipe, preheating grill with all burners set to high and lid down until grill is very hot, about 15 minutes. Use wire brush to scrape clean cooking grate. Leave one burner on high and turn other burner(s) down to medium-low. Cook chicken, covered, over hotter part of grill until well browned, 2 to 3 minutes per side. Move chicken to cooler part of the grill; continue to cook, covered, as directed in master recipe.

Grilled Chicken Breasts with Barbecue Sauce

Any homemade or store-bought tomato-based barbecue sauce will taste great on grilled chicken. Coat the chicken with the barbecue sauce once it is nearly done to prevent the sugars in the sauce from burning. Plan on using about ½ cup of barbecue sauce to coat four split breasts, more if you serve barbecue sauce at the table.

Follow master recipe, making the following changes: About 2 minutes before breasts will be done, brush some barbecue sauce on breasts, turn, and cook for 1 minute. Brush with more sauce, turn, and cook another minute or so. Transfer chicken to serving platter, brush with additional sauce to taste, and serve, with more sauce passed at table if desired.

21

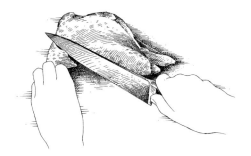

Figure 3.
Trim excess fat or any skin that hangs over the edge of the breast.

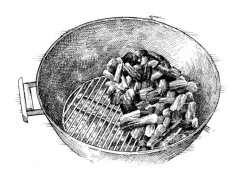

Figure 4.
Thick bone-in breasts are so susceptible to burning on the grill that we pile all the coals onto one side (for searing) and then leave the remaining part of the grill empty (for cooking the breasts through). The intense heat put out by the hot side of the grill is also ideal for quickly cooking boneless cutlets.

Simple Spice Pastes
each makes about 1/3 cup,
enough to coat 4 bone-in, split breasts

➤ NOTE: *Wet and dry ingredients are blended to form two thick pastes.*

Citrus and Cilantro Spice Paste

1	teaspoon ground cumin
1	teaspoon chili powder
1	teaspoon sweet paprika
1	teaspoon ground coriander
2	tablespoons orange juice
1	tablespoon lime juice
1	tablespoon olive oil
1	garlic clove, peeled
2	tablespoons fresh cilantro leaves

Asian Spice Paste

2	tablespoons soy sauce
2	tablespoons peanut oil
1	tablespoon minced jalapeño or other fresh chile, stemmed and seeded
1	tablespoon chopped fresh ginger
1	garlic clove, peeled
2	tablespoons fresh cilantro leaves

II INSTRUCTIONS:

Puree all ingredients for either paste in food processor or blender until smooth. Rub paste over brined and dried chicken breasts before grilling.

Pantry Spice Rub

makes about $1/2$ cup,
enough to coat 4 bone-in, split breasts

➤ **NOTE:** *Other dried spices can be used in a similar fashion. For heat, add some cayenne pepper.*

2	tablespoons ground cumin
2	tablespoons curry powder
2	tablespoons chili powder
1	tablespoon ground allspice
1	tablespoon ground black pepper
1	teaspoon ground cinnamon

II INSTRUCTIONS:

Combine all ingredients in small bowl. Rub mixture over brined and dried chicken breasts before grilling.

GRILLED CUTLETS

Without skin, boneless breasts (cutlets) are especially prone to burning and drying out on the grill. They are more difficult to cook than chicken parts with skin (which keeps in moisture) and bones (which add flavor).

However, many people don't eat chicken skin and would rather not bother with bones. If that's the case, it seems pointless to rub spices into bone-in, skin-on parts and then throw out the skin after cooking. If you don't eat skin, we think you might as well start with boneless, skinless breasts and apply the seasonings where they can be enjoyed.

Our goal was clear: develop a technique for cooking cutlets that would keep these delicate parts as moist as possible. Cutlets have almost no fat and can dry out easily with any cooking method. From our initial tests, it was clear that we needed to get them on and off the grill as quickly as possible. Cooking them over high heat and turning them just once was the best method we tested.

To make the fire quite intense, we spread a full chimney of lit charcoal out over just two-thirds of the grill. The concentrated fire shortened the cooking time by a minute or two. On gas, we just kept the burners on high the whole time and lifted the lid as infrequently as possible.

Although this fast cooking method was delivering good results, we still had some tweaking to do. The area between

25

the tenderloin (the flap of meat at the thick part of the breast) and breast wasn't cooking through. The meat is so thick here that cooking takes a few minutes longer than for the rest of the breast. You have two options: remove the tenderloin, or leave it on and overcook most of the breast just to get the meat underneath the tenderloin cooked through. We opted to remove the tenderloins. Save them for a stir-fry or grill them with the breasts, reducing their cooking time by more than half.

We found it imperative to brush the cutlets with a bit of oil to keep them from sticking to the grill. The oil also helped keep the outer layer of meat from becoming dry and tough.

We had one last test to run: brining. In our initial tests, we used the same brine we had developed for bone-in, skin-on parts. After brining for 1½ hours, the time that works with skin-on breasts, we found that the boneless cutlets were much too salty. After much tinkering, we found that our brine worked in just 45 minutes.

While brined cutlets were juicy and well seasoned, they clearly needed a flavor boost. As with skin-on, bone-in breasts, we found that sticky glazes (such as barbecue sauce) are best applied when the meat is almost cooked through. If applied earlier, the glaze will burn.

Master Recipe

Charcoal-Grilled Chicken Cutlets
serves four

➤ **NOTE:** *Be wary of overcooking, especially if your grill runs hot. To check for doneness with an instant-read thermometer, slide it on an angle into the thickest part of the meat; make sure it does not go entirely through and out the bottom of the meat or the reading will be off.*

¾ **cup kosher salt or 6 tablespoons table salt**

¾ **cup sugar**

4 **boneless, skinless chicken cutlets (about 1½ pounds), tenderloins removed and reserved for another use; fat trimmed (see figure 1, page 12); rinsed and thoroughly dried**

1 **tablespoon extra-virgin olive oil Ground black pepper**

INSTRUCTIONS:

1. Dissolve salt and sugar in 1 quart cold water in gallon-sized, zipper-lock plastic bag. Add chicken breasts; press out as much air as possible from bag and seal. Refrigerate until fully seasoned, about 45 minutes.

27

2. Light large chimney starter filled with charcoal and allow to burn until charcoal is covered with layer of fine gray ash. Build two-level fire by spreading all coals over two-thirds of grill. Set cooking rack in place, cover grill with lid, and let rack heat up, about 5 minutes. Use wire brush to scrape clean cooking grate.

3. Meanwhile, remove chicken from brine, rinse well under cold, running water, and dry thoroughly with paper towels. Toss chicken in medium bowl with oil to coat. Season with pepper to taste.

4. Cook chicken, uncovered, smooth-side down first, directly over hot coals until the chicken is opaque about two-thirds up sides and rich brown grill marks appear, 4 to 5 minutes. Turn and continue grilling until chicken is fully cooked, about 4 minutes. (If using barbecue sauce or one of glazes on page 30 or 31, cook for 3 minutes after turning chicken, brush glaze on both sides, and cook another minute or so, turning once.) To test for doneness, peek into thickest part of chicken with tip of small knife (it should be opaque at the center), or check internal temperature with instant-read thermometer, which should register 160 degrees. Transfer chicken to serving platter. Serve hot or at room temperature.

■■ **VARIATION:**

Gas-Grilled Chicken Cutlets

On a gas grill, cook cutlets over high heat as quickly as possible to keep them moist and juicy.

Follow master recipe, preheating grill with all burners set to high and lid down until grill is very hot, about 15 minutes. Use wire brush to scrape clean cooking grate. Leave all burners on high. Cook chicken, covered, smooth-side down first, until dark brown grill marks appear, about 5 minutes. Turn and continue grilling, covered, until chicken is fully cooked, 4 to 5 minutes. (If using barbecue sauce or one of glazes on page 30 or 31, cook for 3 minutes after turning chicken, brush glaze on both sides, and cook another minute or two, turning once.)

GLAZES FOR CHICKEN CUTLETS

Thick glazes are applied while the chicken cutlets are still on the grill. About two minutes before chicken is cooked through, brush the glaze on both sides of chicken and allow to cook another minute or so on each side.

Homemade or prepared barbecue sauce can be used in the same manner. Use ½ cup barbecue sauce to coat 4 cutlets.

Maple Mustard Glaze
makes about $1/2$ cup,
enough for 4 chicken cutlets

➤ NOTE: *Sharp and sweet, the combination of real maple syrup and whole-grain mustard makes a delicious sweet and sour glaze that can be quickly made while the chicken is cooking on the grill. Because of the high level of sugar in this glaze, make sure to watch the chicken very carefully once the glaze has been applied.*

- ¼ **cup maple syrup**
- ⅓ **cup whole grain mustard**
- 1 **teaspoon balsamic vinegar**

▪ INSTRUCTIONS:

Mix all ingredients together in small bowl. Apply glaze as directed in recipes for charcoal- or gas-grilled cutlets.

Smoky Orange Chile Glaze
makes ¹/2 cup,
enough for 4 chicken cutlets

➤ NOTE: *Chipotle chiles add a smoky, hot flavor to plain chicken breasts. Orange zest and juice, cilantro, molasses, and a touch of lime add sweet and sour notes that balance the heat and smoke of the peppers.*

4	chipotle chiles in adobo sauce, roughly chopped (about 2½ tablespoons), with 2 tablespoons adobo sauce
1	teaspoon grated orange zest
2	tablespoons orange juice
¼	cup lightly packed cilantro leaves
2	teaspoons molasses
3	tablespoons vegetable oil
1	lime, cut into 8 wedges

▪▪ INSTRUCTIONS:

Puree chipotle chiles, adobo sauce, zest, juice, cilantro, and molasses in food processor or blender until smooth. Slowly add oil in thin stream until incorporated. Apply glaze as directed in recipes for charcoal- or gas-grilled cutlets. Serve grilled chicken with lime wedges.

chapter three

3

BROILED
BREASTS

LTHOUGH THEY DON'T SOUND GLAMOROUS, broiled chicken breasts can be great when properly prepared: moist, well-seasoned, with a good caramelized flavor and crisp skin. They can be every bit as good as grilled chicken breasts.

The difficulties with broiling chicken stem from the intense heat put out by the broiler. If the food is placed too close to the heating element, it can char on the outside long before it is cooked through at the center. Getting thin, crisp skin can also be a problem if the skin is not given time to render its fat slowly. To avoid these common problems, we knew we would have to figure out the optimal distance between the oven rack and the heat source as well as the best way to season the meat in order to make it flavorful and moist.

As noted in chapter 1, we found a wide variation in the size of bone-in chicken breasts at the supermarket, with weights ranging from 7 to 14 ounces per breast half. We found that buying breasts of similar size is important to ensure even cooking. We had the best luck with breasts that weighed 10 to 12 ounces; smaller breasts were deemed kind of skimpy (the bones weigh several ounces), and larger breasts were hard to cook through. If broiling breasts of varying size, the best approach is to remove each piece from the oven as soon as it is done.

These early tests showed that broiling, like grilling, is tough on lean breast meat. Clearly, brining would be in order. As expected, the brined breasts were more moist, better seasoned, and, owing to the addition of sugar to the brine, better caramelized. When not brined, the meat is dry and bland by comparison. The rubs and sauces noted in the variations can camouflage some of these problems, but the basic master recipe won't.

We now turned our attention to the actual broiling method. Many recipes suggested broiling chicken parts just 4 to 8 inches away from the heating element. In all cases, the skin burned before the meat was cooked through near the bone. We found that the chicken broiled best when placed on the bottom rack of the oven, some 13 inches from the heating element. At this distance, the meat has time to cook through and the skin won't burn. To caramelize the chicken even more, we moved the broiler pan to the second shelf from the top (about 5 inches from the broiler) for the final minute or two of cooking.

With this information in hand, we realized that broiling bone-in chicken parts is not possible in an old-fashioned stove with the broiler underneath the oven chamber. To get the chicken parts the necessary distance from the heating element, you need a modern oven with the broiler at the top of the main cooking chamber.

Although well browned, the skin was a touch too thick and a bit soggy. Remembering a technique used to cook ducks, we tried slashing the skin a few times before placing it in the oven to broil. This trick worked quite well. The skin rendered a little extra fat and crisped up a bit more. We also discovered that starting the parts skin-side down was key to getting thin, crisp skin. If cooked skin-side up first, the skin tended to become soggy during the final minutes of cooking.

Our broiled chicken was now delicious. In fact, this broiled chicken is as appealing as any grilled chicken, with the benefit of being a year-round recipe.

🦅

Master Recipe

Broiled Bone-In Chicken Breasts

serves four

➤ NOTE: *Though we recommend brining, you can bypass this step if pressed for time; skip step 1 and season the chicken generously with salt and pepper before broiling. This recipe will work only in ovens that have the broiler element in the main chamber. In ovens with a separate broiler underneath the main cooking chamber, it isn't possible to get the chicken breasts far enough away from the heating element. If you are making one of the variations, the ingredients can be prepped while the chicken is brining.*

   ¾   cup kosher salt or 6 tablespoons table salt

   ¾   cup sugar

   4   split chicken breasts (bone in, skin on), 10 to 12 ounces each, excess fat and skin trimmed (see figure 3, page 22)
Ground black pepper

■■ INSTRUCTIONS:

1. In gallon-sized, zipper-lock plastic bag, dissolve salt and sugar in 1 quart cold water. Add chicken and seal bag, pressing out as much air as possible; refrigerate until fully seasoned, about 1½ hours. Remove from brine, rinse well, and dry thoroughly with paper towels.

2. Meanwhile, adjust one oven rack to lowest position and other rack to upper-middle position (top rack should be about 5 inches from heating element; bottom rack should be 13 inches away); heat broiler. Line bottom of broiler pan with foil and fit with slotted broiler-pan top. Following figure 5, page 39, make three diagonal slashes in skin of each chicken piece with sharp knife (do not cut into meat). Season both sides of chicken pieces with pepper and place skin-side down on broiler pan.

3. Broil chicken on bottom rack until just beginning to brown, 12 to 16 minutes. Using tongs, turn chicken skin-side up, and continue to broil on bottom rack until skin is slightly crisp and thickest part of meat registers 160 degrees on an instant-read thermometer, about 10 minutes.

4. Move broiler pan to upper rack. Broil until chicken is dark spotty brown and skin is thin and crisp, about 1 minute. Serve immediately.

Broiled Chicken Breasts with Garlic, Lemon, and Rosemary

Combine 4 minced garlic cloves, 2 teaspoons grated lemon zest, 1 tablespoon minced fresh rosemary leaves, and pepper to taste in small bowl. Combine 3 tablespoons lemon juice and 2 tablespoons extra-virgin olive oil in second small bowl. Follow master recipe, spreading a portion of garlic rub under skin before slashing skin. Brush chicken with lemon juice and oil just before moving chicken to upper rack to crisp skin.

Broiled Chicken Breasts with Jamaican Jerk Dipping Sauce

Stir together ¼ cup lime juice and ¼ cup lightly packed brown sugar until dissolved in small bowl; set aside. Toast 1 unpeeled garlic clove and 1 medium habanero chile in small dry skillet over medium heat, shaking pan frequently, until blistered, about 8 minutes. Peel and mince garlic; seed and mince habanero. Combine garlic, habanero, 2 minced scallions, ½ cup minced onion, 1½ tablespoons minced fresh ginger, ½ teaspoon dried thyme, and pinch ground allspice in second small bowl. Stir in 2 tablespoons lime/brown sugar mixture; set aside as dipping sauce. Follow master recipe, brushing chicken pieces with remaining lime/brown sugar mixture just before moving to upper oven rack to crisp skin. Serve chicken, passing dipping sauce separately.

Deviled Chicken Breasts

The breadcrumb coating can burn if the chicken is moved to the top rack, so the chicken is broiled completely on the lower rack.

Combine 1 tablespoon Dijon mustard, 1 tablespoon white wine vinegar, and ¼ teaspoon cayenne pepper in small bowl; set aside. With fork, mash together 2 tablespoons softened butter and salt and pepper to taste (use salt sparingly if the chicken was brined) in small bowl. Follow master recipe, spreading a portion of the butter under skin before slashing skin. Rub mustard mixture all over chicken breasts. Sprinkle ⅓ cup plain breadcrumbs over skin side of chicken pieces and press to adhere. Carefully place chicken skin-side down on broiler pan and continue with master recipe, omitting step 4.

Five-Spice Broiled Chicken Breasts with Ginger Butter

With fork, mash together 2 tablespoons softened butter, 1 tablespoon minced fresh ginger, and salt and pepper to taste (use salt sparingly if the chicken was brined) in small bowl. Follow master recipe, spreading a portion of the ginger butter under skin before slashing skin. Brush chicken pieces with 1 teaspoon vegetable oil and sprinkle with 2 teaspoons five-spice powder. Carefully place chicken skin-side down on broiler pan and continue with master recipe.

Figure 5.
Make three diagonal slashes in the skin of each breast to help
render fat and promote crispness. Lift the skin up a bit and hold
it taut while cutting. This will keep you from cutting into the
meat and causing juices to be lost during cooking.

chapter four

ROASTED BREASTS & CHICKEN SALAD

OMETIMES YOU WANT THE FLAVOR OF ROASTED chicken but don't have the hour or more needed to cook a whole chicken. Or maybe your family likes roasted chicken, but no one will eat the wings and legs. Roasting bone-in breasts offers a good solution to either problem.

The main challenge when roasting chicken breasts is getting the skin crisp. We like to roast a whole chicken on a basket or V-rack to circulate the heat evenly around the bird and prevent any part of the skin from sitting in fat or cooking juices. We assumed the same thing would hold true for parts, and our tests backed up our hunch. When we roasted parts directly in the pan, the skin was flabbier than when we lifted the parts off the bottom of the pan with a flat rack. You will need a roasting pan large enough to accommodate a flat rack. A 13 by 9-inch roasting pan with fairly shallow sides (about 2 inches high) and a rack that is slightly smaller work especially well.

We next turned our attention to oven heat. We started out using the same temperature we found best for roasting a whole chicken—375 degrees. Given the shorter oven time, we found that the skin did not crisp when parts were cooked at this temperature. Next, we tried 450 degrees. After setting off several smoke alarms, we realized that this superhigh oven heat was going to cause pan drippings to burn. We eventually settled on 425 degrees. At this temperature, the skin was nice and crisp by the time the meat had cooked through. As an added protection against smoking, we found it useful to add one-half cup water to the roasting pan about 15 minutes into the cooking time.

Given the configuration of chicken breasts (the skin is generally on one side, bones on the other), we found no advantage in turning the chicken during the cooking process. Cooking them skin-side up results in the most crispy and best-browned skin. While we found that basting actually makes skin less crisp (coating the skin with liquid and/or fat makes it soggy and slows down the crisping

41

process), we clearly detected a benefit from slipping a little butter under the skin of each piece before cooking. The melting butter helps lift the skin off the meat and causes it to puff up nicely. The butter is also a good medium for herbs, spices, chiles, and other seasonings that can flavor the meat.

Finally, as with grilled or broiled chicken breasts, we like the effect of brining on parts destined for roasting. Although not essential, brining seasons the meat through to the bone and firms up the texture, giving the chicken breasts a meatier taste.

The timing in this recipe will vary depending on the size of the breasts. We found that 7-ounce breasts cooked in 30 minutes, but that 14-ounce breasts took 45 minutes. The best serving size was 10 to 12 ounces. If you have any doubt as to whether the chicken is cooked through, use an instant-read thermometer and pull breasts from the oven once the temperature hits 160 degrees.

☙

Master Recipe

Roasted Bone-In Chicken Breasts

serves four

➤ **NOTE:** *If you're short on time, you can skip brining (step 1) and season the chicken generously with salt. We've found that high heat works best, as it cooks the chicken quickly without drying it out and produces a crisp crust. The only problem comes from the smoking fat at the bottom of the roasting pan. To avoid this nuisance, we pour ½ cup water into the pan 15 minutes into the cooking time.*

- ¾   cup kosher salt or 6 tablespoons table salt
- ¾   cup sugar
- 4   split chicken breasts (bone in, skin on), 10 to 12 ounces each, excess fat and skin trimmed (see figure 3, page 22)
- 2   tablespoons unsalted butter, softened
      Salt and ground black pepper
- 1   teaspoon vegetable oil

▗▖ **INSTRUCTIONS:**

1. In gallon-sized, zipper-lock plastic bag, dissolve salt and sugar in 1 quart cold water. Add chicken and seal bag, pressing out as much air as possible; refrigerate until fully seasoned, about 1½ hours. Remove from brine, rinse well, and dry thoroughly with paper towels.

43

2. Preheat oven to 425 degrees. With fork, mash together butter and salt and pepper to taste (use salt sparingly if chicken was brined) in small bowl. Rub butter mixture under skin of each chicken breast. Place rack in large roasting pan and transfer chicken, skin-side up, to rack. Brush chicken with oil and lightly season with salt and pepper to taste (use salt sparingly if chicken was brined).

3. Roast for 15 minutes. Add ½ cup water to pan to prevent excessive smoking. Cook until juices run clear or internal temperature registers 160 degrees when an instant-read thermometer is inserted into thickest part of breast, another 20 to 30 minutes. Serve immediately.

VARIATIONS:

Roasted Chicken Breasts with Honey Mustard Glaze
Combine ¼ cup Dijon mustard, 2 tablespoons honey, and 1 teaspoon brown sugar in small bowl and set aside. Follow master recipe, brushing chicken with honey mustard glaze when water is added to pan.

Roasted Chicken Breasts with Lemon and Herbs
Follow master recipe, adding 1 tablespoon minced lemon zest and 1 tablespoon minced fresh thyme or rosemary leaves to butter mixture in step 2. Proceed as directed, rubbing lemon-herb butter under skin of each breast.

Roasted Chicken Breasts with Porcini Mushroom Paste

Place 1 ounce dried porcini mushrooms in small bowl and cover with hot tap water. Let stand until mushrooms are soft, about 20 minutes. Carefully lift mushrooms from liquid, pat dry, and chop finely. (Strain and reserve soaking liquid for another use.) Follow master recipe, adding mushrooms, 2 minced garlic cloves, and 2 tablespoons minced fresh parsley leaves to butter mixture in step 2. Proceed as directed, rubbing mushroom paste under skin of each breast.

Roasted Chicken Breasts with Herb Crust

Beaten egg yolks are brushed onto the skin of the chicken pieces to help make the herbs adhere to the skin and to create a nice thick crust. We like the combination of tarragon, parsley, and dill, but mint, cilantro, or even savory can be used in this recipe.

Place 2 cups each loosely packed fresh tarragon leaves, parsley leaves, and dill leaves in work bowl of food processor. Process until finely chopped. Follow master recipe, rubbing butter under skin as directed. Do not brush chicken with oil, but do season with salt and pepper to taste. Brush chicken with 2 lightly beaten egg yolks, sprinkle herb mixture over pieces, and lightly pat herbs so that chicken is evenly coated. Transfer chicken, skin-side up, to oiled rack in roasting pan. Roast as directed in master recipe.

CHICKEN SALAD

Classic chicken salad consists of tender breast meat, pulled apart by hand and bound loosely with mayonnaise. There's a little celery for texture, some parsley or tarragon for flavor, and a squeeze of lemon juice for freshness. We often make this salad from leftover roasted or poached chicken.

So what didn't we know about chicken salad? After a little thought, we had only one question. When making the classic version from scratch, and not from leftover meat, how should we cook the chicken?

Although there were many choices, they basically fell into two camps, wet cooking and dry cooking. The wet cooking methods included poaching, steaming, and roasting in foil (oven-steaming). Chicken cooked by each of these methods had a bland, unmistakably boiled flavor. Roast chicken, which is cooked with dry heat, was a very different matter. The meat tasted roasted and the resulting chicken salad was superb.

Since the skin is to be discarded when roasting breasts for salad, there's no need to elevate the chicken on a rack. It can be cooked directly on the bottom of the roasting pan. You can also get away with a slightly lower oven temperature and thus eliminate the potential for smoking. We found that a little vegetable oil brushed on the chicken helps to keep it moist as it roasts but that butter under the skin makes the meat too rich tasting and not suitable for salad.

Roasted Chicken Breasts for Salad
makes about 5 cups when shredded,
enough for 1 salad recipe

➤ **NOTE**: *Once the chicken breasts have cooled to room temperature, remove and discard the skin. At this point, you may wrap and refrigerate the breasts or make salad.*

2   large whole chicken breasts (bone in, skin on),
      at least 1½ pounds each

1   tablespoon vegetable oil
      Salt

⠿ **INSTRUCTIONS:**

Adjust oven rack to middle position and heat oven to 400 degrees. Set breasts on small, foil-lined jelly roll pan. Brush with oil and sprinkle generously with salt. Roast until meat thermometer inserted into thickest part of breast registers 160 degrees, 35 to 40 minutes. Cool to room temperature, remove skin, and continue with one of the following salad recipes. (Cooked chicken can be wrapped in plastic and refrigerated for 2 days.)

Master Recipe

Creamy Chicken Salad

serves six

➤ **NOTE**: *In addition to the parsley leaves, you can flavor the salad with 2 tablespoons of minced fresh tarragon or basil leaves. You can use leftover meat from a roast chicken, if desired.*

1	recipe Roasted Chicken Breasts for Salad, skinned and boned, meat shredded into bite-sized pieces
2	medium celery ribs, cut into small dice
2	medium scallions, white and green parts, minced
¾	cup mayonnaise
2	tablespoons juice from 1 small lemon
2	tablespoons minced fresh parsley leaves
	Salt and ground black pepper

INSTRUCTIONS:

Mix all ingredients together in large bowl, including salt and pepper to taste. Serve. (Can be covered and refrigerated overnight.)

Waldorf Chicken Salad

Follow master recipe, adding 1 large crisp apple, cored and cut into medium dice, and 6 tablespoons chopped toasted walnuts.

Curried Chicken Salad with Raisins and Honey

Follow master recipe, adding 6 tablespoons golden raisins, 2 teaspoons curry powder, and 1 tablespoon honey. Replace parsley with equal amount of cilantro.

Chicken Salad with Hoisin Dressing

Try serving this Asian-style salad on a bed of young spinach leaves with sliced cucumber and radishes or rolled in a flour tortilla with shredded iceberg lettuce or watercress.

Whisk ⅓ cup rice vinegar, 3 tablespoons hoisin sauce, 1½ tablespoons soy sauce, and 1 tablespoon minced fresh ginger in small bowl. Whisk in 3 tablespoons vegetable oil and 1 tablespoon Asian sesame oil. Follow master recipe, replacing mayonnaise, lemon juice, salt, and pepper with hoisin dressing. If you like, replace parsley with equal amount of cilantro.

chapter five

SAUTÉED CUTLETS

AUTÉING A BONELESS, SKINLESS CHICKEN BREAST
sounds easy. But too often the chicken comes
out only lightly colored and dry. Ideally, a
sautéed chicken breast should have a nicely
browned exterior and a tender, juicy interior.

Although there are several keys to sautéing boneless
chicken breasts successfully, we found that one is para-
mount: There must be enough heat. Home cooks often shy
away from the smoke and splatters that can accompany
strong heat. But a thin, delicate food like boneless chicken
must be cooked through quickly. Cooking over low or even
moderate heat pushes the meat's moisture to the surface

before any browning occurs, and, once the juices hit the exterior of the meat, it will not brown at all, unless it is cooked for a long, long time. Furthermore—and this is especially true for a lean piece of meat such as a chicken breast—these same juices provide the lion's share of moisture; expel them, and the result is a tough, leathery piece of meat rather than a tender, moist one.

There are other points to bear in mind. After you have trimmed excess fat from the cutlets and removed the tendons, rinse them quickly under cool water, then dry the meat thoroughly with paper towels; if the cutlets are wet, they will not brown. For the best flavor, we sprinkle salt and pepper generously on both sides of each cutlet.

We sautéed both floured and unfloured chicken cutlets to see if there would be any differences in taste, texture, or juiciness. We immediately noticed a more dramatic sizzle when the unfloured cutlet hit the pan. While both cutlets sizzled during cooking, the unfloured cutlet "spit" a bit more. The flour seems to provide a barrier between the fat in the pan and the moisture in the cutlet. The floured cutlet was also easier to turn and move in the pan; while neither version stuck to the skillet, the floured cutlet skated easily when we swirled it about.

When cooked, the floured cutlet displayed a consistently brown crust, almost resembling a skin. The uncoated breast was a spotty brown. Both breasts were equally moist, but the floured cutlet had a better mouthfeel with its contrasting crispy exterior and juicy, tender meat. The floured cutlet, reminiscent of fried chicken, was also more flavorful than its uncoated counterpart. Our advice: Flour those cutlets.

In our tests, we found that a 12-inch skillet can comfortably hold four chicken cutlets of about six ounces each (crowded meat will not brown well). Unless the bottom of the pan is reasonably heavy, the chicken will scorch. We tested nonstick and enamel-coated pans and found them perfectly acceptable, but we prefer bare metal—stainless steel or an alloy—as it seems to yield more intense color.

The best cooking medium for chicken cutlets is vegetable oil, which provides excellent browning and won't burn. In a concession to the reigning wisdom about health, we tried sautéing a batch of cutlets in just the sheerest film of oil. The results were disastrous. The oil burned, the outside of the chicken became dry and stringy, and the crust was very disappointing, nearly blackened in some spots and a strange yellowish color in others. For sautéed food to become crisp and uniformly brown, the entire surface must stay in contact with the fat. Meat has an irregular surface, so those parts not in contact with the cooking medium—in this case, the oil—are steamed by the moisture generated by the cooking meat and, therefore, will not brown. For this reason, you will need about two tablespoons of fat in the pan at the start.

Place the oil in the skillet and set the pan over high heat. (While everyone's stove is different, most home burners are quite weak. To get enough heat under the pan to brown the cutlets, you really need to set the burner on *high*.) Once the oil shimmers, quickly add the cutlets, with the tenderloin-side down, holding onto the tapered end as you lay each cutlet down flat.

Maintain the heat at the point where the fat remains at a fast sizzle but does not quite smoke. If you see more than just a wisp or two of smoke, immediately slide the pan off the burner, turn down the heat a bit, and wait a few seconds before returning the pan to the flame. Be advised that there will be some spattering.

♛

Master Recipe

Sautéed Chicken Cutlets

serves four

➤ **NOTE**: *Serve these chicken cutlets with either of the sauces on pages 57–59.*

    4 **boneless, skinless chicken cutlets**
          (about 1½ pounds), fat trimmed and tendons
          removed (see figures 1 and 2, pages 12 and 13);
          rinsed and thoroughly dried
          Salt and ground black pepper
    ¼ **cup all-purpose flour**
    2 **tablespoons vegetable oil**

▒ INSTRUCTIONS:

1. Preheat oven to 200 degrees. Place a plate in oven for keeping cooked cutlets warm while making sauce.

2. Sprinkle both sides of cutlets with salt and pepper to taste. Measure flour onto a plate or pie tin. Working with one cutlet at a time, dredge in flour. Make sure tenderloin is tucked beneath and fused to main portion of breast. Pick up cutlet from tapered end; shake to remove excess flour.

3. Heat heavy-bottomed 12-inch skillet over high heat until

5 4

hot, about 4 minutes. Add oil and heat briefly until it shimmers. Lay cutlets in skillet, tenderloin side-down and tapered ends pointing out (see figure 6, below).

4. Adjust heat to medium-high (fat should sizzle but not smoke) and sauté cutlets, not moving them until browned on one side, about 4 minutes. Turn cutlets with tongs (a fork will pierce meat); cook on other side until meat feels firm when pressed and clotted juices begin to emerge around tenderloin, 3 to 4 minutes. Remove pan from heat and transfer cutlets to warm oven. Continue with one of the sauces that follow.

Figure 6.
To avoid being splashed with hot fat, lay the cutlets into the pan thick-side first and hang onto the tapered end until the whole cutlet is in the pan. The tapered ends of the cutlets should be at the edges of the pan, where the heat is less intense.

PAN SAUCES FOR CHICKEN

The concept of a pan sauce is simple. The juices that escape from the meat (in this case, chicken) during cooking reduce, caramelize, and sometimes harden. The resulting bits, which are basically caramelized proteins that chefs refer to as *fond,* provide a concentrated flavor on which to build a sauce.

To release this flavor into a sauce, a liquid is used to wash and dissolve these bits off the bottom of the pan. This process, known as *deglazing,* can be done with many different liquids, including wine, water, juice, brandy, stock, vinegar, or a combination thereof. The liquid is then boiled and reduced to thicken the sauce. After reducing the liquid, take the pan off the heat and swirl in one or more tablespoons of softened butter to give the sauce added richness and deeper flavor.

If you wish to use butter to thicken a deglazing sauce as well as to enrich its flavor, be sure to observe the following guidelines. The sauce must be slightly syrupy and already well reduced. It takes about 3 tablespoons of butter to thicken ⅓ cup of sauce. Add the butter off the heat and do not return the pan to the heat once the butter has been added; the heat will cause the sauce to separate and thin out. Finally, swirl the pan by the handle, or stir very gently, until the butter is incorporated and the sauce thickened. Note that acidic deglazing sauces—those made with a high proportion of lemon juice, vinegar, or wine—are more stable and thicker than others.

Lemon-Caper Sauce (Piccata)
enough for 4 chicken cutlets

➤ **NOTE:** *Lemon slices and lemon juice give this sauce a strong lemon flavor.*

- **2** **large lemons**
- **2** **tablespoons minced shallot or 1 teaspoon minced garlic**
- **1** **cup chicken stock or canned low-sodium broth**
- **2** **tablespoons drained small capers**
- **2** **tablespoons minced fresh parsley leaves**
- **3** **tablespoons unsalted butter, cut into 3 pieces, softened**

INSTRUCTIONS:

1. Cut one lemon in half from pole to pole. Trim fleshy ends from one half of lemon and then cut crosswise into very thin slices; set slices aside. Juice remaining lemon half along with whole lemon to obtain ¼ cup; reserve separately.

2. Follow Master Recipe for Sautéed Chicken Cutlets. Without discarding fat, set skillet over medium heat. Add shallot or garlic to empty pan and sauté until fragrant, about 30 seconds for shallots, 10 seconds for garlic. Add stock and lemon slices, increase heat to high, and scrape skillet bottom with wooden spoon or spatula to loosen browned bits.

Simmer until liquid reduces to about ⅓ cup, about 4 minutes. Add any accumulated juices from chicken, lemon juice, and capers and simmer until sauce reduces again to ⅓ cup, about 1 minute. Remove pan from heat and swirl in parsley and butter until butter melts and thickens sauce. Spoon sauce over chicken and serve immediately.

Marsala Sauce
enough for 4 chicken cutlets

➤ NOTE: *In our testing, we preferred a sweet Marsala to a dry one for the body, soft edges, and smooth finish it gave the sauce.*

2½	**ounces pancetta (about 3 slices), cut into pieces 1 inch long and ⅛ inch wide**
8	**ounces white mushrooms, sliced (about 2 cups)**
1	**medium garlic clove, minced**
1	**teaspoon tomato paste**
1½	**cups sweet Marsala**
1½	**tablespoons lemon juice**
2	**tablespoons minced fresh parsley leaves**
4	**tablespoons unsalted butter, cut into 4 pieces, softened**

∷ I N S T R U C T I O N S :

1. Follow Master Recipe for Sautéed Chicken Cutlets. Without discarding fat, set skillet over low heat. Add pancetta and sauté, stirring occasionally and scraping pan bottom to loosen browned bits, until pancetta is brown and crisp, about 4 minutes. With slotted spoon, transfer pancetta to paper towel–lined plate.

2. Add mushrooms to fat in empty skillet and increase heat to medium-high; sauté, stirring occasionally and scraping pan bottom, until liquid released by mushrooms evaporates and mushrooms begin to brown, about 8 minutes. Add garlic, tomato paste, and cooked pancetta; sauté while stirring until tomato paste begins to brown, about 1 minute.

3. Off heat, add Marsala; return pan to high heat and simmer vigorously, scraping browned bits from pan bottom, until sauce is slightly syrupy and reduced to about 1¼ cups, about 5 minutes. Off heat, add lemon juice and any accumulated juices from chicken. Swirl in parsley and butter until butter melts and thickens sauce. Spoon sauce over chicken and serve immediately.

chapter six

ভ

SAUTÉED
STUFFED CUTLETS

C UTLETS THAT ARE STUFFED AND BREADED ARE special-occasion food. The filling coats the chicken from the inside with a creamy sauce, while the crust makes a crunchy counterpoint.

They can be very good, but these little bundles pose a number of problems for the cook. The filling must be creamy without being runny; flavorful but not so strong that it overpowers the chicken. The crust must be crisp all over, without burnt spots, and it must completely seal in the filling so that none leaks out.

We first focused on the cooking method. We needed to develop a technique that would crisp the exterior without overbrowning it before the center was fully cooked. Deep-frying was the obvious answer, but this option is really better suited to restaurants than home kitchens. We tested roasting, broiling, sautéing, and combinations of these methods. We found that two approaches warranted further exploration: (1) complete cooking in a skillet on the stovetop and (2) stovetop browning followed by roasting.

We ran our next test on the stove, sautéing the breasts in just enough vegetable oil to generously coat the bottom of a sauté pan. This test revealed a number of problems. First, it was difficult to arrive at a heat level that would cook the chicken through without burning it. Also, the cutlets often stuck to the pan. Furthermore, even though the breasts in the pan at any one time were of only slightly different weights, their rates of cooking were different enough to be a problem.

It seemed logical that the two-step method—a preliminary pan-frying on top of the stove, followed by roasting in the even heat of the oven—would solve the twin problems of overbrowning and undercooking. We sautéed the next batch in oil that came one-third to halfway up the sides of the chicken, cooking until the chicken was well-browned all over. Then, to combat the sogginess we had observed in roasted breasts during the initial round of testing, we baked the chicken on a rack in a jelly roll pan so that hot air could circulate underneath the breasts.

The results were much improved: the breasts didn't stick

to the pan; they came out of the oven evenly browned, with an excellent, crunchy coating; and the meat inside was not soggy but instead almost uniformly moist, with only the skinny tips of the breasts slightly dry. Because the time in the oven didn't significantly darken the crust, we could rely on this method for a perfect crust every time as long as we carefully supervised the stovetop browning.

Next we had to figure out what ingredients to use in the crust. We found that a classic à l'anglaise breading (dipping the cutlets in flour, then in eggs beaten with a little oil and water, and finally in bread crumbs) worked best.

Satisfied with the coating and cooking methods, we turned our attention to the stuffing. During our first round of testing, we had found "pocket-stuffed" breasts to be particularly troublesome. This method calls for slicing horizontally into the thickest part of the cutlet and sandwiching the filling into the middle. Because the filling is placed in the thickest part of the breast, its shape becomes even more uneven. In the oven, this unevenness causes the small tapered end to dry out long before the thicker portion is cooked. And, of course, when you cut into it, the tapered end is disappointingly devoid of filling. Pounding the breasts thin and rolling them up around the filling produced the most even distribution of filling and the most even cooking of the meat. It was also the only method that kept the filling from leaking out during cooking. Once cooked, the breasts could be sliced crosswise into medallions that looked lovely on the plate.

As for the content of the filling, we wanted something creamy but thick. Cheese was the obvious choice. After several tests, we concluded that beaten cream cheese provided the creamy consistency we wanted; it was thick and smooth. For flavor, we turned to more potent cheeses, such as cheddar and Gorgonzola, along with seasonings such as browned onions, garlic, and herbs.

But there was still a problem. These breasts had to be secured with toothpicks—sometimes multiple toothpicks in a single breast—all of which then had to be removed before the breast was sliced into medallions.

Getting over this hurdle turned out to be easier than we anticipated. We reasoned that chilling the stuffed breasts before cooking would inhibit the filling from melting so quickly and that the chilled cheese filling would hold the rolls together. We were right on both counts. Wrapping the breasts in plastic and refrigerating them for one hour before breading and cooking cooled the cheese enough to hold the roll together. It also kept the cheese from seeping out of the crust during baking. Another advantage of this technique is that it allows the cook to prepare the breasts up to this point and refrigerate them overnight.

Master Recipe

Sautéed Stuffed Chicken Cutlets

serves four

➢ **NOTE:** *The chicken breasts can be filled and rolled in advance, then refrigerated for up to 24 hours.*

    4   **boneless, skinless chicken cutlets (5 to 6 ounces each), tenderloins removed and reserved for another use; fat trimmed (see figure 1, page 12); rinsed and thoroughly dried**
        Salt and ground black pepper
    1   **recipe filling (pages 68–69)**
    ½   **cup all-purpose flour**
    2   **large eggs**
  1½   **teaspoons plus ¾ cup vegetable oil**
  1½   **teaspoons water**
    1   **cup plain bread crumbs**

⠿ INSTRUCTIONS:

1. Place each chicken cutlet on large sheet of plastic wrap, cover with second sheet, and pound with meat pounder or rolling pin until ¼ inch thick throughout (see figure 7, page 66). Each pounded breast should measure roughly 6 inches wide and 8½ inches long. Cover and refrigerate while preparing filling.

2. Place breasts smooth-side down on work surface; season with salt and pepper. Fill, roll, and wrap each breast (see figures 8 and 9, page 67). Refrigerate until filling is firm, at least 1 hour.

3. Adjust oven rack to lower-middle position; heat oven to 400 degrees. Spread flour in pie plate or shallow baking dish. Beat eggs with 1½ teaspoons vegetable oil and 1½ teaspoons water in second pie plate or shallow baking dish. Spread bread crumbs in third pie plate or shallow baking dish. Unwrap chicken breasts and roll in flour; shake off excess. Using tongs, roll breasts in egg mixture; let excess drip off. Transfer to bread crumbs; shake pan to roll breasts in crumbs, then press with fingers to help crumbs adhere. Place breaded chicken breasts on large wire rack set over jelly roll pan.

4. Heat remaining ¾ cup oil in medium skillet over medium-high heat until shimmering, but not smoking, about 4 minutes; add chicken, seam-side down, and cook until medium golden brown, about 2 minutes. Turn each roll and cook until medium golden brown on all sides, 2 to 3 minutes longer. Transfer chicken rolls, seam-side down, to wire rack set over jelly roll pan; bake until deep golden brown and instant-read thermometer inserted into center of each roll registers 155 degrees, about 15 minutes. Let stand 5 minutes before slicing each roll crosswise into 5 medallions; arrange on individual dinner plates and serve.

Figure 7.
Place each trimmed cutlet between two sheets of plastic wrap.
Starting in the center of each breast, pound evenly out toward
the edges, taking care not to tear the flesh.

Figure 8.
Place each cutlet, smooth-side down, on work surface, season, and spread with one-quarter of cheese mixture.

Figure 9.
Roll up each cutlet from the tapered end, folding in the edges to form a neat cylinder. To help seal the seams, wrap the stuffed cutlets in plastic and twist the ends of the wrap in opposite directions.

Ham and Cheddar Cheese Filling
enough to stuff 4 breasts

➤ N O T E : *If desired , substitute Gruyère or Swiss for the cheddar.*

- 1   tablespoon unsalted butter
- 1   small onion, minced
- 1   small garlic clove, minced
- 4   ounces cream cheese, softened
- 1   teaspoon chopped fresh thyme leaves
- 2   ounces cheddar cheese, shredded (about ½ cup)
     Salt and ground black pepper
- 4   thin slices cooked deli ham

I N S T R U C T I O N S :

1. Heat butter in medium skillet over low heat until melted; add onion and sauté, stirring occasionally, until deep golden brown, 15 to 20 minutes. Stir in garlic and cook until fragrant, about 30 seconds longer; set aside.

2. In medium bowl, using hand mixer, beat cream cheese on medium speed until light and fluffy, about 1 minute. Stir in onion mixture, thyme, and cheddar; season with salt and pepper and set aside. To stuff breasts, place one slice ham on top of cheese on each breast, folding ham as necessary to fit onto surface of breast.

6 8

:: VARIATIONS:

Gorgonzola Cheese Filling with Walnuts and Figs

Two tablespoons of dried cherries or cranberries can be substituted for the figs.

Follow recipe for Ham and Cheddar Cheese Filling, replacing cheddar cheese with 2 ounces crumbled Gorgonzola cheese (about ½ cup). Stir in ¼ cup chopped toasted walnuts, 3 medium dried figs, stemmed and chopped (about 2 tablespoons), and 1 tablespoon dry sherry along with Gorgonzola. Omit ham.

Broiled Asparagus and Smoked Mozzarella Filling

To cook asparagus for this filling, toss trimmed spears with 2 teaspoons olive oil and salt and pepper to taste on a jelly roll pan, then broil until tender and browned, 6 to 8 minutes, shaking pan to rotate spears halfway through cooking time.

Follow recipe for Ham and Cheddar Cheese Filling, replacing cheddar cheese with 2 ounces shredded smoked mozzarella cheese (about ½ cup). Replace ham with 16 medium asparagus, trimmed to 5-inch lengths and broiled. Place 4 asparagus spears horizontally on top of cheese on each breast, spacing them about 1 inch apart and trimming off ends if necessary.

chapter seven

BAKED CUTLETS

EALTH CONSIDERATIONS ASIDE, SAUTÉING is our preferred method for cooking a chicken cutlet. The thick, brown crust and tender, juicy interior cannot be duplicated by any other cooking method. Grilling is a good low-fat alternative to sautéing (see chapter 2), but there are no pan juices with which to make a sauce. In many cases, it is the pan sauce that makes bland cutlets worth eating. Also, grilling is not always an option.

We identified two lower-fat options for cooking boneless chicken cutlets: baking in an open pan and enclosing the cutlets and seasonings in parchment paper or foil packets and then baking, or "steaming," the chicken in the oven.

BAKED CHICKEN CUTLETS

We decided to focus first on baking the cutlets in an open pan. (For information on oven-steaming, see page 80). We wanted to develop a technique that could be used year-round and that would also give us some precious pan juices. From the start, we knew this would be a tough assignment. Roasting a piece of meat that contains almost no fat presents an obvious challenge: how to keep it moist and juicy.

Many traditional recipes for baked chicken cutlets call for lots of butter and cream to keep the meat moist. While this undoubtedly works, the results are generally not as good as they are when similar dishes are made on the stove; the chicken does not brown when it sits in a bath of heavy cream. We think the oven makes sense only when there is a desire to keep the fat content to a minimum.

With that goal in mind, we started testing a number of variables—especially the temperature of the oven and the use of ingredients (other than cream) that might keep the chicken moist as it bakes. It was soon apparent that getting the chicken in and out of the oven as quickly as possible is key. The longer it stays in the oven, the drier it gets. High temperatures (we settled on a constant 450 degrees) cook the cutlets quickly and prevent dryness. Baking cutlets in a hot oven also causes some browning, which boosts flavor in what is otherwise a fairly bland piece of meat.

Roasting chicken cutlets at a high temperature is only part of the answer. The meat still tends to dry out, especially in spots where the cutlets are thin and toward the exterior. We needed to give the cutlets enough time to cook through in the center while protecting the outside layer of meat from becoming tough. It was clear that we needed to add moisture and, yes, a little fat. Adding a bit of oil (one-half tablespoon per cutlet) helps create the impression of moistness in the outer layer of meat and also promotes browning. Since cutlets are so bland, we use olive oil to add flavor as well.

We also found that liquids from moist vegetables, such as tomatoes and mushrooms, are essential in keeping the chicken from becoming tough and dry. Our testing showed that placing the vegetables both underneath and on top of the chicken was the best guarantee of moistness in the end. While the vegetables don't affect the interior of the cutlet, their juices do flavor and moisten the exterior layer, which is so prone to drying out in the oven.

We found that tomatoes could be treated differently from other vegetables, such as onions, mushrooms, fennel, and peppers. Tomatoes are so juicy and soften so quickly that they can go into the oven at the same time as the chicken. When using the other vegetables, we found it best to roast them first to bring their juices to the surface, then add the cutlets to the pan and continue baking until everything was tender. This two-stage cooking process (without and then with the chicken) lets harder vegetables soften up properly. When we put onions or peppers into the oven right along with the chicken, they would still be crunchy when the chicken was done. Therefore, we created two master recipes: one that covers the chicken with raw tomatoes and another that roasts vegetables first, then adds the chicken.

Bold flavorings also turned out to be key to our oven-baked dishes. Even if the meat is juicy, without seasonings, it's really not worth eating. Spices, garlic, and herbs all help. We also found brining of the breasts to be worth the minimal effort required. In fact, brining has a more pronounced effect on cutlets than it does on skin-on, bone-in breasts because in the latter the skin and bones contribute flavor and moisture. Even with the protective effects of juicy vegetables, unbrined cutlets will be a tad dry in spots when baked.

If you don't have time to brine, use smaller cutlets, which will cook through fairly quickly and spend minimal time in the oven. When we neglected to brine larger cutlets, we found them dry, especially in the outer layers.

We realized that our efforts had produced an unintended side effect. By baking chicken with vegetables as a protective measure, we had also created a nearly complete meal. With the addition of a leafy salad or a starch, dinner was done.

♛

Master Recipe

Baked Chicken Cutlets with Tomatoes and Herbs

serves four

➤ NOTE: *Brining does improve the flavor and texture of the cutlets, but if you are short on time, skip step 1 and add salt to the parsley mixture.*

¾   cup kosher salt or 6 tablespoons table salt

¾   cup sugar

4   boneless, skinless chicken cutlets
    (about 6 ounces each), fat trimmed and tendons
    removed (see figures 1 and 2, pages 12 and 13);
    rinsed and thoroughly dried

¼   cup chopped fresh parsley leaves

¼   teaspoon cayenne pepper (optional)

2   medium garlic cloves, minced very fine
    Salt and ground black pepper

2   tablespoons extra-virgin olive oil

½   teaspoon dried oregano

2   cups cored and chopped fresh plum tomatoes
    (about 6 tomatoes) or drained and chopped
    canned tomatoes

∷ INSTRUCTIONS:

1. In gallon-sized, zipper-lock plastic bag, dissolve salt and sugar in 1 quart of water. Add chicken and seal bag, pressing out as much air as possible; refrigerate until fully seasoned, about 45 minutes. Remove from brine, rinse well, and dry thoroughly with paper towels.

2. Preheat oven to 450 degrees. Combine parsley, cayenne, garlic, pepper, and salt (omit if chicken was brined) in small bowl. Rub chicken all over with herb mixture.

3. Combine oil, oregano, tomatoes, and salt and pepper to taste in medium bowl. Spoon half of tomato mixture into 13 by 9-inch roasting pan. Place chicken on top and cover with remaining tomato mixture.

4. Roast until chicken is cooked through, 15 to 20 minutes, basting once or twice with pan juices. To check for doneness, cut into thickest part of one breast with small knife. If there is any hint of pink, return chicken to oven till done. Serve immediately.

∷ VARIATIONS:

Asian-Style Baked Chicken Cutlets
with Tomatoes and Herbs

Follow master recipe, making the following changes:

Substitute ¼ cup chopped fresh cilantro for parsley. Add 1 tablespoon minced fresh ginger to cilantro mixture. Replace oregano with 4 thinly sliced scallions.

Baked Chicken Cutlets with Tomatoes and Porcini Mushrooms

Dried Italian porcini mushrooms lend richness but not fat to baked chicken breasts. A little of their soaking liquid is added to the pan for moisture. Any other dried mushrooms, especially morels or shiitakes, may be substituted.

Place 1 ounce dried porcini mushrooms in medium bowl and cover with hot tap water. Let mushrooms soak until softened, about 20 minutes. Carefully lift mushrooms from liquid, pat dry, and finely chop. Strain soaking liquid through sieve lined with paper towel. Reserve ¼ cup strained soaking liquid for this recipe, saving the rest for another use. Follow master recipe, making the following changes: Substitute ¼ cup chopped fresh basil leaves for parsley. Omit cayenne and oregano. Add mushrooms and reserved soaking liquid to tomato mixture.

Master Recipe

Baked Chicken Cutlets with Roasted Onions and Mushrooms

serves four

➤ **NOTE:** *Roasted vegetables provide the moisture that keeps cutlets moist as they bake. Roast the vegetables partway, add the chicken, and continue baking until both the vegetables and chicken are done. Brining does improve the flavor and texture of the chicken, but if you are short on time, skip step 1 and add salt to the thyme mixture.*

¾	cup kosher salt or 6 tablespoons table salt
¾	cup sugar
4	boneless, skinless chicken cutlets (about 6 ounces each), fat trimmed and tendons removed (see figures 1 and 2, pages 12 and 13); rinsed and thoroughly dried
2	medium onions, halved and sliced thin
10	ounces white button or cremini mushrooms, ends trimmed and sliced thin
2	tablespoons extra-virgin olive oil
	Salt and ground black pepper
2	tablespoons chopped fresh thyme leaves
2	medium garlic cloves, minced very fine

77

⁘ INSTRUCTIONS:

1. In gallon-sized, zipper-lock plastic bag, dissolve salt and sugar in 1 quart of water. Add chicken and seal bag, pressing out as much air as possible; refrigerate until fully seasoned, about 45 minutes. Remove from brine, rinse well, and dry thoroughly with paper towels.

2. Preheat oven to 450 degrees. Combine onions, mushrooms, oil, and salt and pepper to taste in 13 by 9-inch roasting pan. Roast, stirring once or twice, until onions begin to brown and mushrooms give off their juices, 15 to 20 minutes.

3. Meanwhile, combine thyme, garlic, pepper, and salt (omit if chicken was brined) in small bowl. Rub chicken all over with herb mixture.

4. Transfer half of onions and mushrooms from roasting pan to bowl; spread remaining vegetables evenly over bottom of pan. Place chicken on top of onions and mushrooms and then cover with onions and mushrooms in bowl.

5. Roast until chicken is cooked through, 15 to 20 minutes, basting once or twice with pan juices. To check for doneness, cut into thickest part of one breast with small knife. If there is any hint of pink, return chicken to oven till done. Serve immediately.

■■ VARIATIONS:

Baked Chicken Cutlets with Roasted Peppers and Onions

Follow master recipe, replacing mushrooms with 2 medium red, yellow, and/or orange bell peppers, cored, seeded, and cut into ½-inch-thick strips.

Baked Chicken Cutlets with Roasted Fennel and Tomatoes

Follow master recipe, replacing onions and mushrooms with 2 cups thinly sliced fennel (about 1 medium bulb) and 2 cups cored and chopped plum tomatoes (about 6 medium), and reducing roasting time in step 2 to 15 minutes. Proceed as directed, replacing thyme with 1 tablespoon chopped fresh oregano leaves.

OVEN-STEAMED CHICKEN CUTLETS

Cooking *en papillote* is a classic French technique that involves oven-steaming fish, chicken, or vegetables in parchment paper packets. The food cooks in its own juices and stays especially moist. We tested parchment paper and heavy-duty aluminum foil packets and found no difference in the end results. Although parchment packets do look intriguing and are pretty enough to slice open at the table, foil is easier to find and work with and is our first choice.

Like baked cutlets, oven-steamed cutlets need a little liquid to keep them juicy. The liquid also becomes an instant sauce when the chicken is cooked. In our testing, we found that these recipes require no oil at all as long as liquid is added to the packets in the form of juicy vegetables and wine. In addition, heavy seasonings (don't stint on the salt and pepper) and the use of flavorful ingredients (especially garlic and herbs) are necessary to keep oven-steamed chicken from being too bland. No browning or caramelization can occur when chicken is cooked in foil packets, so bold seasonings are a must.

Brining makes a big difference in the quality of oven-steamed cutlets; they were much juicier and more flavorful than those which had not been brined. If not brining, we recommend using smaller cutlets to minimize cooking time, which will help keep the meat from drying out.

Since the chicken is actually cooking in its own juices (plus a little wine and vegetable juices), the packages must not be opened until the cooking is done. If opened too soon, the built-up steam is released and the chicken is not as moist when done. For this reason, bake the packets by weight—at least 20 minutes for cutlets that are six ounces or fewer and 25 minutes for cutlets that are particularly thick or weigh much more than six ounces each. When you bring the packets to the table, you can rest assured that they will be cooked through but still juicy.

This chicken is best eaten immediately after cooking. The meat emerges from the oven moist and tender, but as soon as it cools the texture begins to become drier and tougher. When preparing this recipe, it is critical to put a stop to cooking the moment the chicken is removed from the oven. To do so, open all packages immediately.

Master Recipe

Oven-Steamed Chicken Cutlets with Tomatoes and Herbs

serves four

➤ **NOTE**: *This technique for oven-steaming cutlets is similar to that used for baking them. There are just a few changes. White wine replaces the olive oil and everything—the chicken, vegetables, and seasonings—is enclosed in foil packets before baking.*

¾ cup kosher salt or 6 tablespoons table salt

¾ cup sugar

4 boneless, skinless chicken cutlets (about 6 ounces each), trimmed and tendons removed (see figures 1 and 2, pages 12 and 13); rinsed and thoroughly dried

¼ cup chopped fresh parsley leaves

¼ teaspoon cayenne pepper (optional)

2 medium garlic cloves, minced very fine
Salt and ground black pepper

2 cups cored and chopped fresh plum tomatoes or drained and chopped canned tomatoes

¼ cup white wine

INSTRUCTIONS:

1. In gallon-sized, zipper-lock plastic bag, dissolve salt and sugar in 1 quart of water. Add chicken and seal bag, pressing out as much air as possible; refrigerate until fully seasoned, about 45 minutes. Remove from brine, rinse well, and dry thoroughly with paper towels.

2. Preheat oven to 450 degrees. Combine parsley, cayenne, garlic, pepper, and salt (omit if chicken was brined) in small bowl. Rub chicken all over with herb mixture.

3. Cut 4 pieces of heavy-duty aluminum foil about 12 inches square. Arrange portion of tomatoes in center of each piece of foil. Top with one chicken breast. Drizzle 1 tablespoon wine over each breast and fold foil to make packets (see figures 10 through 12, pages 84–85).

4. Put foil packets on rimmed baking sheet and bake 20 to 25 minutes. Open packets, taking care to keep steam away from your hands and face. Transfer contents of packets to individual plates and serve immediately.

▞ VARIATIONS:

You can adapt any of the baked cutlet recipes for oven steaming as follows: Rub chicken with seasonings. Place all vegetables on foil, but omit oil. Top with chicken and drizzle with 1 tablespoon wine. Wrap all ingredients in foil packets and bake as directed in step 4, above. (There's no need to roast vegetables separately.)

Figure 10.
Arrange vegetables and seasoned cutlet in center of 12-inch sheet
of heavy-duty aluminum foil. Drizzle wine over chicken, then
bring the sides of the foil up to meet over the chicken.

84

Figure 11.
Crimp the edges together in a ¼-inch fold, and then
fold over three more times.

Figure 12.
Fold the open edges at either end of the packets together in a
¼-inch fold, and then fold over twice again to seal. When
opening the packets after baking, take care to keep steam away
from your hands and face.

chapter eight

STIR-FRIED CUTLETS

T O STIR-FRY PROPERLY YOU NEED PLENTY of intense heat. The pan must be hot enough to caramelize the sugars and proteins in the meat, deepen flavors, and evaporate unnecessary juices. All this must happen in minutes. The problem for most American cooks is that the Chinese wok and the American stovetop are a lousy match that generates moderate heat at best.

Woks are conical because in China they traditionally rest in cylindrical pits containing the fire. Food is cut into small pieces to shorten cooking time, thus conserving fuel. Only one vessel is required for many different cooking methods, including sautéing (stir-frying), steaming, boiling, and deep frying.

Unfortunately, what is practical in China makes no sense in America. Stovetop cooking, in which heat comes at the pan only from the bottom instead of from all sides, doesn't work with a wok. On an American stove, the bottom of the wok gets hot but the sides become only warm. A horizontal heat source requires a horizontal pan. Therefore, for stir-frying at home, we recommend a large skillet, 12 to 14 inches in diameter, with a nonstick coating. If you insist on using a wok for stir-frying, choose a flat-bottomed model. It won't have as much flat surface area as a skillet, but it will work better on an American stove than a conventional round-bottomed wok.

American stoves necessitate other adjustments. In Chinese cooking, intense flames lick the bottom and sides of the wok, heating the whole surface to extremely high temperatures. Conventional stoves simply don't generate enough British Thermal Units (BTUs) to heat any pan (whether a wok or flat skillet) sufficiently for a proper stir-fry. American cooks must accommodate the lower horse-power on their stoves. Throw everything into the pan at one time and the ingredients will steam and stew, not stir-fry.

One solution is to boil the vegetables first so that they are merely heated through in the pan with the other stir-fry ingredients. We find this precooking to be burdensome. After testing, we found that we could avoid precooking by following two strategies. First, cut the vegetables quite small; second, add them to the pan in batches. By adding a small volume of food at a time, the heat in the pan does not dissipate. Slow-cooking vegetables such as carrots and onions go into the pan first, followed by quicker-cooking items such as zucchini and bell peppers. Leafy greens and herbs go in last.

The other option, which works best with green vegetables, is to steam them in the pan. Just stir-fry them in a little oil, add some water, and cover the skillet. Once the broccoli, green beans, or asparagus have cooked, they should be removed from the skillet to prevent color loss or overcooking. Return these vegetables to the pan just before adding the cooked chicken and sauce.

We find it best to freeze chicken for an hour or so to making slicing easier. We tried several kinds of marinades and found that a simple mixture of soy sauce and dry sherry is best. Just make sure to drain the protein before stir-frying. If you add the marinating liquid, the chicken will stew rather than sear.

Many stir-fry recipes add the aromatics (scallions, garlic, and ginger) too early, causing them to burn. In our testing, we found it best to add the aromatics after cooking the vegetables. When the vegetables are done, we push them to the sides of the pan, add a little oil and the aromatics to the center of the pan, and cook briefly until fragrant but not colored, about 10 seconds. To keep the aromatics from burning and becoming harsh-tasting, we then remove the pan from the heat and stir them into the vegetables for 20 seconds. Then the seared chicken is added back to the pan along with the sauce.

A good stir-fry for four people needs only ¾ pound of chicken to 1½ pounds of prepared vegetables. This ratio keeps the stir-fry from becoming too heavy and is also more authentic, since protein is a luxury used sparingly in China.

As for the sauces, we have kept the ingredient lists quite simple. We find that a few strongly flavored and carefully chosen ingredients can do the job. We tried thickening sauces with cornstarch but found that it made the sauces gloppy and thick. Without any thickener, they were cleaner tasting and brighter. Just make sure the pan is very hot when you add the sauce so that excess moisture can evaporate, causing the sauce to thicken slightly.

Master Recipe

Stir-Fried Chicken and Broccoli with Hoisin Sauce

serves four

➤ **NOTE:** *The secret to this classic stir-fry dish is lots of heat, so preheating the pan is crucial. After cooking the chicken, steam the broccoli in the same skillet over medium heat. When the broccoli is tender but still crisp, remove it to a plate to prevent further cooking. Turn the heat back to high and finish this dish in a sizzling hot skillet. If you like your stir-fries hot and spicy, add ¼ teaspoon of hot pepper flakes to the pan with the garlic, ginger, and scallions.*

¾	pound boneless, skinless chicken cutlets, fat trimmed and tendons removed (see figures 1 and 2, pages 12 and 13); rinsed and thoroughly dried; cut into uniform pieces (see figures 13 through 15, pages 94–95)
1½	tablespoons light soy sauce
1	tablespoon dry sherry
3	tablespoons hoisin sauce
2	tablespoons chicken stock or low-sodium canned broth
1	teaspoon Asian sesame oil
4	tablespoons peanut oil

90

1¼   pounds broccoli, florets broken into bite-sized
      pieces; stems trimmed, peeled, and cut on
      diagonal into ⅛-inch-thick ovals

⅓   cup water

2   cups sliced shiitake mushrooms (about 4 ounces)

1   tablespoon minced garlic

1   tablespoon minced fresh ginger

2   tablespoons minced scallions, white parts only

▓ I N S T R U C T I O N S :

1. Toss chicken with 1 tablespoon soy sauce and sherry in medium bowl; set aside, tossing once or twice.

2. Mix remaining ½ tablespoon soy sauce with hoisin sauce, chicken stock, and sesame oil in small bowl; set aside.

3. Heat a 12- or 14-inch nonstick skillet over high heat for 3 to 4 minutes. Drain chicken. Add 1 tablespoon peanut oil to pan and swirl so that it evenly coats pan bottom. Heat oil until it just starts to shimmer and smoke. Add chicken and stir-fry until seared and three-quarters cooked, about 2½ to 3 minutes. Scrape cooked chicken and all liquid into clean bowl. Cover and keep warm.

4. Let pan come up to temperature, about 1 minute. When hot, add 1 tablespoon peanut oil and swirl so that it evenly coats bottom of pan. When oil just starts to smoke, add broccoli and stir-fry for 30 seconds. Add water, cover pan, and lower to medium heat. Steam broccoli until crisp-tender, about 2 minutes. Transfer broccoli to plate lined with clean kitchen towel.

5. Let pan come up to temperature, about 1 minute. When hot, add another tablespoon peanut oil and swirl so that it evenly coats bottom of pan. When oil just starts to smoke, add shiitake mushrooms and stir-fry until golden, about 2 minutes. Clear center of pan and add garlic, ginger, and scallions, drizzle with remaining tablespoon of peanut oil, and stir-fry until fragrant but not colored, 10 to 15 seconds. Add broccoli back to pan, remove pan from heat, and stir scallions, garlic, and ginger into vegetables for 20 seconds.

6. Return pan to heat and add cooked chicken along with its liquid, stir in sauce, and stir-fry until ingredients are well coated with sauce and sizzling hot, about 1 minute. Serve immediately.

⚏ VARIATIONS:

Stir-Fried Chicken and Green Beans with Garlic Sauce

Follow master recipe, making the following changes: In step 2, omit hoisin sauce, increase soy sauce to 2 tablespoons, and add 1 tablespoon sherry and ½ teaspoon sugar to soy sauce, chicken stock, and sesame oil. Substitute 1¼ pounds string beans for broccoli and increase steaming time in step 4 to about 4 minutes. Replace mushrooms with 1 five-ounce can sliced water chestnuts and decrease cooking time in step 5 to 30 seconds. Increase garlic to 2 tablespoons.

Stir-Fried Chicken and Bok Choy with Ginger Sauce

Bok choy does not need to be steamed—simply stir-fry it.

Follow master recipe, making the following changes: In step 2, omit hoisin sauce, increase soy sauce to 2 tablespoons, and add 1 tablespoon sherry and ½ teaspoon sugar to soy sauce, chicken stock, and sesame oil. Replace broccoli with 1 pound bok choy, stalks and greens separated and cut into thin strips. In step 4, stir-fry bok choy stalks in 1 tablespoon oil for 1 to 2 minutes. Add 1 red bell pepper, stemmed, seeded, and cut into 3 by ½-inch strips and cook 1 minute. Add bok choy greens and cook 15 to 30 seconds. Omit mushrooms and the tablespoon of oil used to stir-fry them in step 5. Continue with step 5 of the master recipe by clearing the center of the pan and adding the garlic, 2 tablespoons ginger, and scallions.

9 3

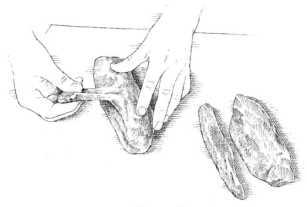

Figure 13.

Slightly frozen meat is easier to slice thinly than meat at room temperature. Place the chicken in the freezer for one hour to firm up its texture, or slice frozen chicken that has been partially defrosted. To prepare chicken cutlets for a stir-fry, start by removing the tenderloins. Set them aside.

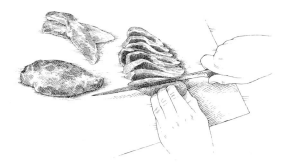

Figure 14.

Slice the main part of the cutlet across the grain into ½-inch-wide strips that are 1½ to 2 inches long. The center pieces will need to be cut in half so that they are approximately the same length as end pieces.

Figure 15.

Cut the tenderloins on the diagonal to produce pieces about the same size as the strips of breast meat.

i n d e x